© 2019 by Robbie Daymond

All rights reserved. This book or any portion thereof may not be reproduced or used in any manner whatsoever without the express written permission of the publisher except for the use of brief quotations in a book review.

Printed in the United States of America

First Printing, 2019

www.robbiedaymond.com

For Lynnyx,

You are the shining light in the darkness.
Burn bright and fill up their hearts.

Lynnie & Lug
vs. THE FOREST

Written by **Robbie Daymond**   Illustrated by **Faryn Hughes**

Her Mom always said she'd be a great engineer,
But sadly her Mother is no longer here.
For so many months it's been Lynnie alone,
It feels like this cabin is all that she's known.

She remembers the day everyone disappeared.
Her Mom said, "Lynn, we have to get out of here!"

They came to the woods, to Grandpa's old cabin.
Mom thought Grandpa might come, (but that never happened).
Soon they ran out of food, so Mom left with her pack.
She said "Love you, Lynn," but she never came back.

Lynnie cried for weeks
because her Mother was gone,
Yet soon she realized
that life had to go on.
Perhaps she was hungry,
alone and afraid,
But Mom would want her to
live and try to be brave.

She'd found a book in the cabin, "How to Survive in the Wild,"
though somehow she thought it wasn't written for a child.
She foraged for berries, got fresh veggies to grow,
Caught a few fish for dinner, but let the squirrels go.

She thought to herself, "I might just be alright,"
Until she got lost in the forest one night...

She made it back to the cabin
not a minute too soon.
Outside in the night the Dark Things loomed.
Instead of crying or hiding or freezing with fright,
Lynnie secured the cabin and locked it up tight.

That night she thought hard how to make this all end,
Then it came in a flash! "I have to build a friend!"

She needed a partner who was big and strong,
Who could fight by her side, but still sing her a song.
He'd be made out of steel and seven feet tall!
And his face would be gentle, not scary at all.

Lynnie read and she studied,
crafting her plan,
Until it was time to build
her own Metal Man.

She went back to the warehouse
when the sun first came up,
Scavenged all her parts
(plus a new coffee cup!)

Back at the cabin she built a workshop,
Where she started to
tinker and hammer and chop.
There were circuits for
splicing and metal for welding,
Lynnie found it exciting,
not a bit overwhelming.

She spent her nights working with skill and detail,
Sometimes she'd succeed, other times she would fail.

The questions were tough, or the books were just wrong.
A tool wouldn't work, a wire didn't belong.

It was the hardest thing Lynnie had ever done,
But she never gave up and even had some fun.

After lots of hard work,
determination and grit,
It was time to see if the final piece fit.

With a wrench she tightened
the very last bolt,
And her creation came alive
with a "ZAP" and a jolt!

Had she programmed him right?
Worked out all the bugs?
He knelt down to her...

And gave her one great big hug!

"Nice to meet you,"
she whispered, clutching his frame;
"I'm Lynnie," she said,
"But now you need a name."

The robot stood and stretched to the roof,
And one of his shiny lug nuts rattled loose.
"That's it!" she exclaimed, fixing the part.
"I'll call you Lug!" and lights glowed in his heart.

He could be silly or dance and Lynnie would beam,
A girl and her robot, a natural team!
Days were full of excitement and work to be done,
But they always came back with the setting sun.

That night she dreamt of
leaving their cabin for two,
And sometimes dreams have ways
of making themselves come true.

The next day they relaxed for the first time in weeks. Lynnie read by the river while Lug oiled his squeaks.

Suddenly his antenna shot straight up to the sky! It had never worked, though Lynnie'd certainly tried!

A voice came from Lug's speaker,
"Is anyone there?!"
"I am!" said Lynnie.
Silence hung in the air.

They searched for a signal, but no one replied.
Lug's antenna stayed down no matter how hard they tried.
They'd searched far and long, it was almost dusk.
Creatures stirred in the shadows, the air filled with musk.

They got to the cabin just a little too late.
The door stood wide open, glowing eyes laid in wait.
"Let's go," said Lynnie "but my map and my pack!"
The smile in Lug's eyes seemed to say, "Be right back."

The two emerged from the woods at the top of a hill,
The cabin behind them, the forest now still.
Before them the sun shined on a quaint little town,
A little too quiet, with no one around.

Suddenly Lug's antenna shot straight up and spun,
The two smiled at each other and started to run.

Lynnie had done it, built a robot best friend.
Their adventure's just starting, but for now, it's...

The End

ABOUT THE AUTHOR

Robbie Daymond is a steadfast storyteller and entertainer by nature. After completing his M.F.A. in acting, he moved to Los Angeles to pursue a career in performance and writing. As a prolific voice-artist and actor, he has voiced hundreds of characters in western animation, anime, commercials, film, television, audiobooks and videogames. Though he has worked as a writer in other areas, this is his first children's book, and he is absolutely thrilled and grateful that you decided to read it. (So are his wife, Megan; their daughter, Lynnyx; and the family pets – Zelda, the dog, and Link, the cat.) He and his fantastic family spend their days in Los Angeles and love exploring their big, beautiful city. Robbie hopes to continue to tell stories – whether they be in a sound booth, on stage or screen, or on the page – for as long as he has an audience that will enjoy the tales.

ABOUT THE ILLUSTRATOR

Faryn Hughes is an illustrator from St. Paul, Minnesota. She graduated from the University of Minnesota Twin Cities in 2014 with a Bachelor's Degree in studio art and illustration. Faryn specializes in ethereal watercolor works inspired by nature scenes, animal wildlife, and storybooks. Visual storytelling is her artistic passion. She loves illustration that creates an immersive atmosphere and whimsical narrative. Her previous projects have been for books, editorial illustration, and concept art. Faryn has illustrated multiple published children's books and has worked for national editorial clients such as The New York Times.

CPSIA information can be obtained at www.ICGtesting.com
Printed in the USA
LVIW011003261119
638567LV00002B/3